THE GROTESQUE ALPHABET

of

Jan Christian Bierpfaff

(ca.1650)

Libellus Novus

Elementorum

Latinorum

engraved by
Jeremias Falck

THEOPHANIA PUBLISHING

The Libellus Novus Elementorum Latinorum is a series of ornate letterform prints blending a grotesque botanical styling with an unusual abstract baroque ornamental form. The prints were designed by Polish goldsmith Jan Christian Bierpfaff (1600-1690), and engraved by Jeremias Falck (1610–1677).
Bierpfaff apprenticed with the Mackensen family of metalworkers in Kraków. The Mackensen clan introduced the Dutch Auricular style of ornament, featuring "Ear-like, or Shell-like" patterns, from which this collection has drawn inspiration from, and which was to become a popular style in competing Polish gold and silver workshops. The design is fluid and whimsical, expressing itself with floral and gargoyle forms dynamically hidden within its letterforms.

This exquisite facsimile is presented as a design resource for artists of all crafts, and admirers of interesting and odd typology and print matter.

Libellus Novus
Elementor:m Latino-
rum Cum Aneis pictu-
ris usui Aurifabro-
rum inservientib.
Invenit et edidit
Joh. Christian Bierpfaf
S. R. M. Pol. et Svec
Aurifaber Aulicus
Nunc Civis Thorunen.
Sculpsit
Jeremias Falck
Hamburgi.
Spectabili et
Ingeniosis Viro.
Dn. Andrea Makensen Civi
et Aurifabro Gedanensi
Amico suo observanter
colendo dedicat Autor

J.G.B in:
J.T. Sculp

J.C.B. in: J.F. Sculp:

J.C.B. in. J.F. Sculp.

J.P.B. in:
J.F. Sculp:

J.C.B. in.
J.F. Sculp:

J.C.B. in:
J.F. Sculp:

J.C.B. in:
J.F. Sculp:

I. C. B. in
I. F. Sculp:

J.C.B in:
J.F. Sculp

J.C.B. in.　　　J.F. Sculp.

J.C.B. in:
J.F. sculp:

J.C.B in:
J.F. Sculp:

J. C. Bie. in: J F. Sculp.

J. C. B. in:
J. F. Sculp:

J. C. B in:
J. F. sculp.

J. C. B. in.
J. F. Sculp.

J.C.B. in.
J.F. Sculp:

J. C. B. in:
J. F. Sculp:

J.C.B. in:
J.F. Sculp:

I.G.B. in.
I.T. Sculp.

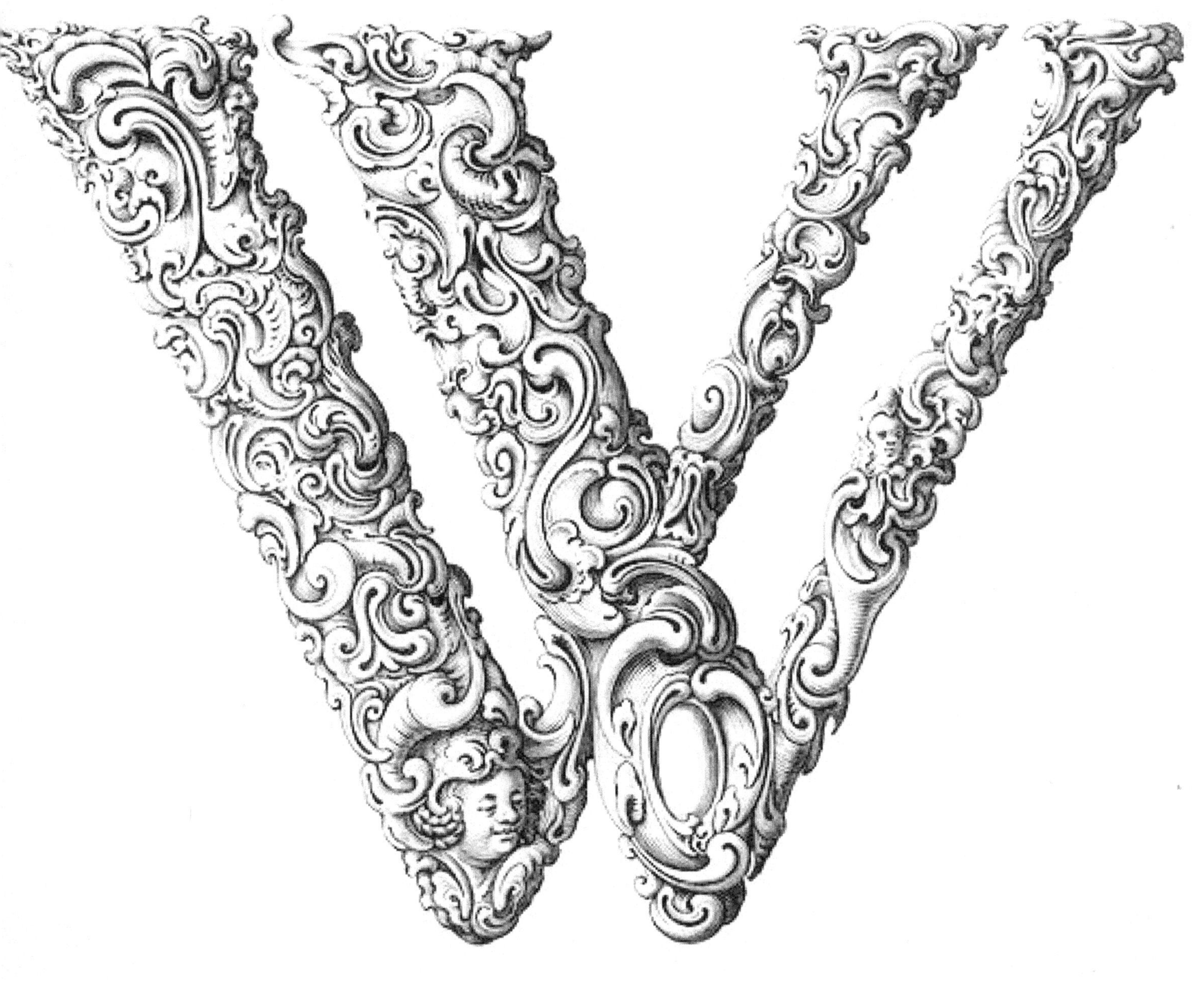

I.C.B. in.
I Falck sculp.

J. C. B. in:
J. F. Sculp:

J.C.B: in:
J.F. sculp: